Workbook

Fo

D1738571

The Light We Carry

(A Guide To Michelle Obama's Book)

A Powerful Guide For Overcoming The Toughest Times Of Life

Kendrick Moore

Copyright © 2022 Kendrick Moore

DISCLAIMER

This is an independently published workbook by Kendrick Moore written to serve as an effective and life changing guide to Michelle Obama's book. Please bear in mind that this is in no way an officially endorsed workbook by Michelle Obama and should not be confused, mistaken, misinterpreted or considered as a replacement for Michelle Obama's Book.

SECTION ONE

Staying Hopeful And Calm In The Present Challenging World

*T*here is no doubt that we as humans seem to be encountering more challenges in this modern day world than it used to be. It is however natural for us humans to feel a sense of fear and anxiety in times of challenges but in order to overcome these feelings and not let it take charge of us we need to be optimistic and stay positive. Everyone in life including Michelle Obama experiences challenges but what sets each one of us apart from the rest is our ability to withstand *these challenges and not let it affect us negatively.*

How hopeful and calm we are in the midst of challenges is greatly dependent on how focused and quiet our brain and senses are on the challenges we're facing. Put these things into practice:

- *Write down all those challenges you're facing (mainly the ones you are capable of handling} and figure out an action plan of how you intend to tackle them.*

- *Each time it seems like your mind is beginning to get overburdened by challenges, don't panic, sit comfortably at a place, **breath in, out, in and out again.** Doing this for as little as 10 minutes will have an* *unbelievable effect in helping you relieve yourself of stress.*

- *Make positive declarations in your life each morning you wake up. Say words to yourself like **"it will be better," "I will overcome,"** e.t.c*

- *Practice the habit of mindfulness meditation every morning you wake up. You can achieve this by:*

  1. *Ensuring that your environment is quiet such that you can hear the sound of a pin drop. You can either stay in your house or relocate to an entirely different area as long as the place is calm and peaceful*

  2. *Sit in a comfortable or relaxed position*

  3. *While meditating, allow thoughts to enter and pass*

through without allowing yourself to focus on those thoughts

4. *Practice this for at least 10 minutes while ensuring that you remain calm and focused all through the meditation*

Personal Notes

....
....
....
....
....
....
....
....
....
....
....
....
....

....
....
....
....
....
....
....
....
....
....
....
....
....
....
....
....
....
....
....
....
....
....
....
....
....
....

....
....
....
....
....
....
....
....
....
....
....
....
....
....
....
....
....
....
....
....
....
....
....

Our mind is capable of generating numerous thoughts that if not properly handled can result into great misery, suffering and untold sadness.

However, you can practice the following to remain positive amidst all this recurring thoughts of the mind

- *Write down all those challenges you're currently experiencing that is beyond your control in the space below*
- *Write out the self-care routines which you can effectively manage and set out a time schedule for them*
- *Go out, share your problems with friends and loved ones and seek for solutions. You may be surprised that your problem is far less than theirs.*
- *Write down all those challenges you can control and rank them*

in order depending on how big the challenge is.

- *Tackle each of this challenges bit by bit. You don't have to kill or overstress yourself while tackling these challenges.*

Personal Notes

....
....
....
....
....
....
....
....
....
....
....
....
....
....
....
....
....

....
....
....
....
....
....
....
....
....
....
....
....
....
....
....
....
....
....
....
....
....
....
....
....
....
....
....
....

....
....
....
....
....
....
....
....
....
....
....
....
....
....
....
....
....
....
....
....
....
....
....
....
....
....
....
....
....

Some of us quickly resort to isolation the moment we find ourselves facing challenges. But Isolation isn't the solution because most times it ends up making matters worse. Put these things into practice:

- *When you're facing any challenge and it's beginning to seem unbearable, reach out to others for support. The people you're to reach out to can be your friends, family members as well as professional support*

- *When telling others about your problems, be honest and don't keep things to yourself. You'll realize that the moment you share your problems with others, it will be as though a heavy burden has been lifted from you. Remember the saying which goes* ***"a problem***

shared is a problem half solved."

- *Try and get access to all the support and emergency services in your community. You can make inquiries from others to access them*

Personal Notes

....
....
....
....
....
....
....
....
....
....
....
....
....
....
....

....
....
....
....
....
....
....
....
....
....
....
....
....
....
....
....
....
....
....
....
....
....
....
....
....
....
....

....
....
....
....
....
....
....
....
....
....
....
....
....
....
....
....
....
....
....
....
....
....
....
....
....
....
....

Showing love to others and acting positively can play a great role in helping you cope with challenges. Put these things into practice.

- *Stop always thinking only about your own personal desires and interest.*
- *Go out and find someone you can help no matter how little it might be.*
- *Write down how you feel within you each time you offer any little assistance to others in the space below*

Personal Notes

....
....
....
....
....
....
....

....
....
....
....
....
....
....
....
....
....
....
....
....
....
....
....
....
....
....
....
....
....
....
....
....
....
....
....
....

....
....
....
....
....
....
....
....
....
....
....
....
....
....
....
....
....
....
....
....
....
....
....
....
....
....

There are series of activities and routines which replenish and help you regain your sense of happiness each time time it is as though you're beginning to feel drained and overburdened by challenges. Put these activities into practice.

- *Write out those activities that make you happy such that each time you engage in them, you tend to forget about the challenges you're facing. These activities or routines could be music, sight-seeing, singing, dancing, playing football, e.t.c. Write them down in the space below*
- *Map out a convenient time daily to perform these activities. (make sure you do them consistently)*
- *Find friends, neighbors or family members to follow you engage in these activities. It could be more fun doing so*

Personal Notes

....

....

....

....

....

....

....

....

....

....

....

....

....

....

....

....

....

....

....

....

....

....

....

....

....
....
....
....
....
....
....
....
....
....
....
....
....
....
....
....
....
....
....
....
....
....
....
....
....
....
....
....

There are sometimes when as a result of the challenges we face in life, we begin to feel restless, distracted, numb and anxious which now makes it necessary for us to be calm. Put these routines into practice in order to actualize this calmness.

- *Practice deep relaxation practices such as mindfulness meditation practices like yoga and others (make it a daily routine)*
- *Map out a convenient time table for engaging yourself in exercise. This exercise can be swimming, cycling, playing football, e.t.c*
- *Share your problems with individuals who will give you a deep listening ear and show you the way forward out of your problems*

- *Practice routines or exercises that permits deep relaxation. If you're unsure of how to do this on your own, you can search and register for online services that teaches the best ways for practicing these routines.*

Personal Notes

....
....
....
....
....
....
....
....
....
....
....
....
....
....
....
....

....
....
....
....
....
....
....
....
....
....
....
....
....
....
....
....
....
....
....
....
....
....
....
....
....
....
....
....

....
....
....
....
....
....
....
....
....
....
....
....
....
....
....
....
....
....
....
....
....
....
....
....
....
....
....

SECTION TWO

Building and Establishing Honest Relationships In The Face Of hallenges

*ost times, our ability to successfully navigate through the challenges we face in life is solely dependent on our support network that is to say the people we surround ourselves with. A simple act of encouragement from a friend, family member or neighbor in the midst of challenges can be all that we need to overcome these challenges afterall if we have that realization that **we are not alone** in the challenges we face and decide to work as a team in tackling these challenges, it reduces the burden we face both emotionally, physically and otherwise thus keeping us in a very* *sound shape to face these challenges. Building good relationships have repeatedly been shown to greatly improve our happiness, health and reduce stress in the midst of challenges. It has also repeatedly been proven that people with good relationships are often more happy, hopeful, calm, more relaxed and more optimistic in the face of challenges. There are several ways of meeting and establishing good connection and relationships with the right people who will stand firmly by you in the face of challenges.*

EXERCISE

Some of us have unnecessarily high and unrealistic expectations when trying to establish relationships with others. This mentality however doesn't always prove to be helpful on the long run. Ask yourself these questions and be very honest in your self-examination.

- *Do I set very high standards or high expectations for people I intend to be my friends?*
- *Do I accept people for who they are or what I intend to benefit from them?*
- *Do I allow others to be themselves or do I try manipulating them into doing things they don't intend doing?*
- *Do I judge people a lot?*

- *Do I believe in sharing my problems with others or do I feel too proud to share my problems with others?*
- *Do I believe in team spirit?*
- *Do I underrate the problem solving ability of others in the face of challenges?*
- *Do I select my friends based on social status, race, gender and other segregator factors?*

Practice This: Whenever you're making friends, bear in mind that you should keep your mind open to accepting people and liking them for who they are. No more people you accept into your life, the more you build your support network in the face of challenges.

Personal Notes

....
....
....
....
....
....
....
....
....
....
....
....
....
....
....
....
....
....
....
....
....
....
....
....

....
....
....
....
....
....
....
....
....
....
....
....
....
....
....
....
....
....
....
....
....
....
....
....
....
....

Some of us don't have the habit of dialoguing with our friends in the midst of challenges. Communication is essential to building great relationships in the midst of challenges. Put these things into practice.

- *Always be there for your friend whenever he needs you. Don't give excuses or reasons why you're not gonna listen to his or her problems. Be attentive and lend a listening ear to him or her. They will reciprocate your good deeds when you face your own difficulties*
- *When your friend(s) is/are sharing problems with you, listen attentively such that all your senses will be focused on whatever your friend is telling you. Don't interrupt what*

they're saying or allow your attention to be diverted by your phone, social media or whatever you're doing. Listen attentively to understand what they're saying and maintain a good body language

- *Ask your friend(s) who is experiencing challenges helpful and encouraging questions that shows that you're truly concerned about them. Ask them questions such as:*

1. *How have you been coping with your experiences?*
2. *Hope it's not making you feel too bad, depressed or demoralized?*
3. *What do you think is the best way to help you overcome this situation?*

4. How much will be enough to help you come out of this problem (if it is financial)

Note: In all this ensure that you're genuine and eager to help your friend tackle these problems and that all this is reflected in your body language.

Personal Notes

....
....
....
....
....
....
....
....
....
....
....
....
....
....
....

....
....
....
....
....
....
....
....
....
....
....
....
....
....
....
....
....
....
....
....
....
....
....
....
....
....
....
....

....
....
....
....
....
....
....
....
....
....
....
....
....
....
....
....
....
....
....
....
....
....
....
....
....
....
....
....

Our ability to establish honest relationships in the face of challenges is greatly dependent on how honest and genuine we are in sharing relevant information about ourselves right from day one. Ask yourself these questions:

- *Am I normally willing and ready to share relevant information about myself such as my name, where I come from, e.t.c with others?*
- *Am I too secretive, security conscious or suspicious of others?*
- *Am I free minded with relating the events of my life with my friends?*
- *Am I straight forward in my relationship with others*

Please Note: *Be open and free-minded with sharing information about yourself with others but don't share too much personal information at a time.*

Personal Notes

....
....
....
....
....
....
....
....
....
....
....
....
....
....
....
....
....
....
....
....
....

....
....
....
....
....
....
....
....
....
....
....
....
....
....
....
....
....
....
....
....
....
....
....
....
....
....
....

....
....
....
....
....
....
....
....
....
....
....
....
....
....
....
....
....
....
....
....
....
....
....
....
....
....
....

In as much as we initially tend to feel insecure with people most especially those we just met, it is necessary to create room for growth in relationships so as to build a solid support network in the face of challenges. Put these into practice

- *Be tolerant with the difference in attitude of your friends and their varying view and opinions about issues even if it does not go in line with your own ideology. Always bear in mind that all humans are not the same*
- *Go and establish constant communication with friends most especially the new ones in order to know each other better*
- *Always be ready to live your comfort zone and make sacrifices for your friends as*

long as it will help the friendship to grow.

- *Don't be too rigid or over-principled when relating with others*

- *Don't be too judgmental or highly sensitive to the weakness of others. Be ready to tolerate any mistakes they make and see it as a normal part of life.*

Personal Notes

....
....
....
....
....
....
....
....
....
....
....
....

....
....
....
....
....
....
....
....
....
....
....
....
....
....
....
....
....
....
....
....
....
....
....
....
....
....
....
....

....
....
....
....
....
....
....
....
....
....
....
....
....
....
....
....
....
....
....
....
....
....
....
....
....
....

*In as much as it is necessary to build healthy relationship with others so as to increase your support network in times of challenges, it is very important to have a good relationship with **yourself** and ensure that the other person whom you care about also cares about you.*

Put these into practice:

- *Make a critical assessment of your friends to discover the ones who are selfish, greedy, exploitative and do not add any value in your life*
- *Detach yourself from this kind of friends*
- *Give your friends only the assistance that is in your power to go. Don't stress yourself beyond your limit*

47

- *Ensure that the care you, your friends and other members of your support network is mutual*
- *In as much as you or your friends are passing through any form of challenges, always make out time to take care of yourself.*

Personal Notes

....
....
....
....
....
....
....
....
....
....
....
....
....
....
....

....
....
....
....
....
....
....
....
....
....
....
....
....
....
....
....
....
....
....
....
....
....
....
....
....
....
....
....

....
....
....
....
....
....
....
....
....
....
....
....
....
....
....
....
....
....
....
....
....
....
....
....
....
....
....
....

Many of us are not trustworthy, dependable and responsible which makes it difficult to establish good relationships that will be beneficial most especially in challenging times.

Ask yourself these questions:

- *Do I disappoint people so often?*
- *Do I take things for granted no matter how serious it is?*
- *How many people can I confidently say that has trust in me?*
- *Am I someone who stands by my words?*

Please Note: *Your ability to makes plans or agreements with someone and stick to that agreement goes a long way in helping you build a solid support network with others that will* *be highly beneficial to you in times of challenges.*

Personal Notes

....
....
....
....
....
....
....
....
....
....
....
....
....
....
....
....
....
....
....
....
....
....

....
....
....
....
....
....
....
....
....
....
....
....
....
....
....
....
....
....
....
....
....
....
....
....
....
....
....
....

Most times, in our existing relationship with people, we tend to quarrel, disagree or fallout with one another. This doesn't however mean you don't like each other and can't support each other in challenging times.

Put these into practice:

- *Each time you have any disagreement or confrontation with your friend(s) make sure you all dialogue or settle the matter afterward. (This dialogue should be done when you're in a lighter or better mood)*
- *Don't always portray yourself as the angel or the one who is always right*
- *If your friend offended you or behaved badly, address the bad*

behavior not his/her personality.

- Never use the "always" or "never" language to address the issue you're having with your friend. For instance **"you never call me on phone," "you're always insulting me,"** e.t.c

- Whenever you're having any misunderstanding, check yourself critically, if you're the one at fault, apologize.

- Always be open to communication or dialogue so as to be able to understand people better and not pass quick judgments.

Please Note: Remember that not all difficulties or differences can be resolved. We're all different and have values, beliefs, habits and personalty

*that may not always be in agreement
with each other's own.*

Personal Notes

....
....
....
....
....
....
....
....
....
....
....
....
....
....
....
....
....
....
....
....
....
....
....

....
....
....
....
....
....
....
....
....
....
....
....
....
....
....
....
....
....
....
....
....
....
....
....
....
....
....

In as much as we can for one reason or another tend to disagree with each other, one rate of disagreement should be far less than our rate of positive or happy interactions.

Put these in practice:

- *Figure out and write down those most common factors that has in the past led you into disagreement with others in the space given*
- *Always give praise and compliments to others from time to time*
- *Never make anyone feel bad, cheated or less than the other.*

Write the results of your practice in the space below

Personal Notes

....
....
....
....
....
....
....
....
....
....
....
....
....
....
....
....
....
....
....
....
....
....
....
....
....
....
....

....
....
....
....
....
....
....
....
....
....
....
....
....
....
....
....
....
....
....
....
....
....
....
....
....
....
....
....

In as much as maintaining very good relationship with others is highly beneficial in times of challenges, It cannot satisfy all our needs and desires. There is some satisfaction which only you and you alone can provide for yourself. Put these into practice.

- *Write out those activities which you're always so passionate and excited about in the space given*
- *Map out a convenient time schedule for practicing these activities*
- *Make sure that your relationship with others is not restraining or stopping you from doing what you love doing*
- *Always be yourself.*

Personal Notes

....
....
....
....
....
....
....
....
....
....
....
....
....
....
....
....
....
....
....
....
....
....
....
....
....
....
....

....
....
....
....
....
....
....
....
....
....
....
....
....
....
....
....
....
....
....
....
....
....
....
....
....
....
....

So many people are normally in a rush to establish relationships with others but in the actual sense, establishing healthy relationships that will be beneficial in challenging times is a process that requires a lot of patience.

Ask yourself these questions:

- *Am I sociable?*
- *Am I desperate and always in a hurry when it comes to making friends?*
- *Do I really know much about my friends?*
- *How did I meet my friend(s)*
- *Can I confidently say that my friends are people who can help me in challenging times?*

Personal Notes

....

....

....

....

....

....

....

....

....

....

....

....

....

....

....

....

....

....

....

....

....

....

....

....

....

....

....
....
....
....
....
....
....
....
....
....
....
....
....
....
....
....
....
....
....
....
....
....
....
....
....
....
....

SECTION THREE

Overcoming Feelings Of Helplessness And Uncertainty In Of Challenges

*M*any people in the face of challenges suddenly begin to feel helpless and uncertain whether things will ever get better. Michelle Obama and many other successful people who in one way or the other faced challenges did not allow the challenges to overcome them but rather than being helpless and uncertain, found hope and strength in the midst of challenges.

The feeling of helplessness and uncertainty most especially in our modern world filled with great challenges is something that many individuals experience at one time or the other. It is a feeling that results from challenging and traumatic times. This feeling if not properly handled can lead to depression and other problems.

The feeling of helplessness can make one lose motivation to change or liberate his/herself from the challenging situation.

However, this practical routines I'm about to walk you through will help you overcome these feelings of helplessness and enable you stay positive and motivated to tackle your challenges.

EXERCISE

When you begin to feel that there is absolutely nothing you can do to come out of the challenging situation, it can be of great necessity to do some personal evaluation of what the source of the situation is in the first place. Ask yourself these questions:

- *What is the origin or source of my problem?*
- *Have I been recently coping with high level of stress?*
- *Have I experienced any form of trauma and setback recently?*
- *Is there any occurrence in the world that is outside my country?*
- *Apart from the feelings of **uncertainty** and **helplessness,** have I been struggling with other feelings such as sadness,*

*loss of interest and others
which might be connected?*

*Please Note: Analyzing, examining
and identifying the factors that might
be contributing to your feeling of
helplessness and uncertainty can help
you decide on the strategy that is most
helpful to you.*

*Write your honest evaluation of
yourself in the space provided.*

Personal Notes

....
....
....
....
....
....
....
....
....

....
....
....
....
....
....
....
....
....
....
....
....
....
....
....
....
....
....
....
....
....
....
....
....
....
....
....

....
....
....
....
....
....
....
....
....
....
....
....
....
....
....
....
....
....
....
....
....
....
....
....
....
....
....
....

Most times, when we start experiencing the feeling of helplessness and uncertainty in the face of challenges, we discover that we automatically begin to resist any attempt to become empowered. However, you need to make a dramatic change in the way you approach life in order to stop the feeling of helplessness.

Put these into practice:

- *Critically analyze and figure out some of the reasons why you might be resisting feeling empowered.*
- *Weigh the alternative provided in order to liberate from "helplessness," even if it might be challenging, still go for that alternative*

73

- *Always be ready and willing to make a big change in your overall perception of life*
- *Change your mindset and the overall way you view your challenges*

Personal Notes

....
....
....
....
....
....
....
....
....
....
....
....
....
....
....
....

....
....
....
....
....
....
....
....
....
....
....
....
....
....
....
....
....
....
....
....
....
....
....
....
....
....
....

....
....
....
....
....
....
....
....
....
....
....
....
....
....
....
....
....
....
....
....
....
....
....
....
....
....
....
....

Most times, we tend to focus all our attention on the challenges which we can't control thus making us feel more helplessness and uncertain in the face of these challenges. Adopt the following approach:

- *Write down all the challenges you might be currently facing*
- *From what you have written, analyze your situation and figure out those challenges which you can't control*
- *Separate them from the ones you can control*
- *Focus all your attention towards tackling/finding solution to those challenges you can control*

Personal Notes

....
....
....
....
....
....
....
....
....
....
....
....
....
....
....
....
....
....
....
....
....
....
....
....
....

....
....
....
....
....
....
....
....
....
....
....
....
....
....
....
....
....
....
....
....
....
....
....
....
....
....
....
....

There are sometimes when our thoughts tend to deceive us and cause us to believe things that are wrong. These wrong thoughts can play a great role in the way we view our challenges thus making us feel hopeless and hopeless. This wrong pattern of thoughts by the brain can be referred to as **Cognitive distortions.**

Put these strategies into practice:

- *Whenever you find yourself feeling helpless with thoughts such as* **"It's never going to get better," "There is nothing I can do to tackle this situation,"** *and other negative thoughts going through your mind, pause for a while, critically analyze and take a more realistic view of the situation.*

- *Observe and try to recognize whenever you're following this wrong pattern of thoughts.*

Personal Notes

....
....
....
....
....
....
....
....
....
....
....
....
....
....
....
....
....
....
....
....

....

....

....

....

....

....

....

....

....

....

....

....

....

....

....

....

....

....

....

....

....

....

....

....

....

....

....

....
....
....
....
....
....
....
....
....
....
....
....
....
....
....
....
....
....
....
....
....
....
....
....
....
....
....
....

After recognizing this wrong thought pattern, the next step is to take the bull by the horn (tackle this thoughts of helplessness)

Put these strategies into practice in order to actualize this:

- *Figure out all this wrong thoughts and replace them with more accurate or empowering thoughts*
- *Each time you're harboring helpless thoughts, remember the times when you successfully tackled problems on your own*

Personal Notes

....
....
....
....
....
....
....

....
....
....
....
....
....
....
....
....
....
....
....
....
....
....
....
....
....
....
....
....
....
....
....
....
....
....

....
....
....
....
....
....
....
....
....
....
....
....
....
....
....
....
....
....
....
....
....
....
....
....
....
....
....
....

In the face of any feeling of helplessness you might be experiencing, it is necessary for you to recognize those unique attributes you possess that makes you feel capable of handling any challenges that come your way. Put these into practice.

- *Write down all your unique talents and abilities in the space below*
- *Remember the past events when you must have you these your unique talent to solve problems on your own*
- *Make a list of all the things you're good at doing.*
- *Relate these things you're good at doing to your present challenges and write down how you can them to solve your problem*

Personal Notes

....
....
....
....
....
....
....
....
....
....
....
....
....
....
....
....
....
....
....
....
....
....
....
....
....
....
....

....
....
....
....
....
....
....
....
....
....
....
....
....
....
....
....
....
....
....
....
....
....
....
....
....
....
....
....
....
....

....
....
....
....
....
....
....
....
....
....
....
....
....
....
....
....
....
....
....
....
....
....
....
....
....
....
....

There is no doubt that amidst all the challenges we face, there are actually some of them beyond our control that we have no other choice than to accept them as they are and move on with life. Having that feeling that you are capable of controlling everything can make you feel more helpless and uncertain about the situation.

Put these into practice:

- *Focus on the present challenges you're facing that are within your control.*
- *Practice the habit of **mindfulness** and be consistent about it.*
- *Forget about all those things you can't control and don't stress yourself thinking about it.*
- *Bear in mind that God can solve any challenges you're*

91

facing no matter how big it might be. Always know that with God all things are possible.

- *Always keep hope alive, stay motivated and keep striving till the end. **Once there is life, there is hope.***

Personal Notes

....
....
....
....
....
....
....
....
....
....
....
....
....
....
....

....
....
....
....
....
....
....
....
....
....
....
....
....
....
....
....
....
....
....
....
....
....
....
....
....
....
....

....
....
....
....
....
....
....
....
....
....
....
....
....
....
....
....
....
....
....
....
....
....
....
....
....
....
....

....
....
....
....
....
....
....
....
....
....
....
....
....
....
....
....
....
....
....
....
....
....
....
....
....
....

Additional Notes & Remarks

....

....

....

....

....

....

....

....

....

....

....

....

....

....

....

....

....

....

....

....

....

....

....

....

....

....

....
....
....
....
....
....
....
....
....
....
....
....
....
....
....
....
....
....
....
....
....
....
....
....
....
....

....
....
....
....
....
....
....
....
....
....
....
....
....
....
....
....
....
....
....
....
....
....
....
....
....
....
....

....
....
....
....
....
....
....
....
....
....
....
....
....
....
....
....
....
....
....
....
....
....
....
....
....
....
....

....
....
....
....
....
....
....
....
....
....
....
....
....
....
....
....
....
....
....
....
....
....
....
....
....
....
....

....
....
....
....
....
....
....
....
....
....
....
....
....
....
....
....
....
....
....
....
....
....
....
....
....
....
....
....

Made in the USA
Monee, IL
15 November 2022

17840163R00059